Zombiegate

by Matthew Gabrielli

Published by Playdead Press 2022

© Matthew Gabrielli 2022

Matthew Gabrielli has asserted his rights under the Copyright, Design and Patents Act, 1988, to be identified as the author of this work.

A CIP catalogue record for this book is available from the British Library.

ISBN 978-1-915533-06-7

Playdead Press
www.playdeadpress.com

Zombiegate by Matthew Gabrielli was first presented by Ameena Hamid Productions and Theatre503, on Tuesday 1st November 2022 at Theatre503 with the following cast:

CAST

Sophie	Ebony Jonelle
Jamie	George Howard
Tony / Simon	Chand Martinez
Jennifer / Danielle	Virginia Thompson

CREATIVE

Writer | Matthew Gabrielli

Director | Julian Bruton

Movement & Puppetry Director | Phoebe Hyder

Set & Costume Designer | Delyth Evans

Puppet Maker | Aled Williams

Lighting Designer | Danny Vavrečka

Sound Designer | Hattie North

Production Manager | Misha Mah

Stage Manager | Nikita Bala

Casting Director | Amy Blair for AJB Casting

PR | Flavia Fraser-Cannon for Mobius PR

Producer | Ameena Hamid for Ameena Hamid Productions

Artwork by Rebecca Pitt
Artwork Photography by Michael Wharley
With thanks to **Arts Council England**

Ebony Jonelle | Sophie

Ebony graduated with a BA(Hons) in Acting from the Liverpool Institute for Performing Arts where she was awarded the Andrew Lloyd Webber Scholarship.

Her work in theatre includes: *Les Miserables: Staged Concert* (Sondheim Theatre); *Les Miserables* (UK & Inter'l Tour); *As You Like It* (National Theatre Public Acts / Queens Theatre Hornchurch); *Top Girls* (National Theatre); and *Alice in Wonderland* (Stephen Joseph Theatre).

Television includes: *Intelligence* (Sky). Film includes: *Ma'am* (Short)

Ebony was nominated for the Ian Charleson Award for 'Rosalind' in *As You Like It*

George Howard | Jamie

George trained at Bristol Old Vic Theatre School where he was awarded the Sir John Gielgud Bursary Award. George recently made his screen debut as Ian St Clair in the critically acclaimed series *Sherwood* (BBC One), playing a young David Morrissey.

Stage credits include *Witness For The Prosecution* (London County Hall); *King Lear* directed by Tom Morris (Bristol Old Vic); *Votes For Women* (New Vic); *Playhouse Creatures* (New Vic); *A Comedy Of Errors* (UK Tour); *Mites* (Tristan Bates Theatre); and *The Caucasian Chalk Circle* (Greenwich Theatre).

Chand Martinez | Tony / Simon

Chand is an actor and puppeteer, trained at BBC, RADA, London Mime School, and the Little Angel Theatre. As an actor, he has worked with the BBC, The Royal Court and

Young Vic theatres, Southwark playhouse, lyric Hammersmith and toured with Tara Arts, Kali, Theatre Centre, Young Shakespeare Co, Kazzum, Tutti Fruity, Hit Galamp, Dende, Cornish Theatre collective, Strangeface and the Big Picture Company. He has operated and built puppets for CBBC, Kazzum, the Little Angel and the Royal Court theatres and performed in Puppetry festivals in Edinburgh, Beverly and Tunbridge Wells as well as numerous summer fairs and fetes with Strangeface. He is currently developing shows with Strangeface and his own projects.

Virginia Thompson | Jennifer / Danielle

Virginia Thompson trained at The Royal Academy of Dramatic Art. She will be appearing in this year's Christmas film *Walk out to Winter* for Sky. Some of her TV credits include; *EastEnders*, *My Family*, *Inspector Lynley Mysteries*. She also appeared in this year's revival of *Small Island* at the National Theatre.

Matthew Gabrielli | Writer

Matthew Gabrielli is a writer for stage, screen and funding applications, he was a winner of Theatre Royal Haymarket's Masterclass Pitch Your Play 2018. Originally from the North-West and now based in Birmingham his short plays have been performed in fringe venues in Manchester, Liverpool and across the Midlands. In 2021 he created the immersive theatre experience *The Lapworth Experiment* (The Lapworth Museum of Geology) and was one of Graeae's Beyond Artists.

Julian Bruton | Director

Julian graduated with a BA (Hons) in Drama and Theatre Practice at the University of Hull. He has directed at venues including Theatre Royal Haymarket, Southwark Playhouse,

Theatre Royal Stratford East, Old Red Lion Theatre, Camden People's Theatre, and Theatre503. He was selected as one of the directors for The 24 Hour Plays UK in 2020.

Previous productions as Director include *Letters to Morrissey* (Mountview); *HOT MESS* (Lion and Unicorn); *Laughing Wild* and *The Man* (University of Hull)

Previous productions as an Assistant Director include *HAMM: Perfectly Processed Education* (RADA Festival); *Free* (Southwark Playhouse); *The Pillowman*, and *Call Me, Love Me* (University of Hull).

Phoebe Hyder | Movement and Puppetry Director

Phoebe is an Actor, Puppeteer, Movement Director, Puppetry Director and Movement Artist specialising in Mocap/Pcap. She is a member of The MDA and within a movement and puppetry capacity has been made a Jermyn Street Theatre Creative Associate for 22/23. Since graduating from GSA in 2017 on the Sir Micheal Redgrave scholarship, Phoebe has gone on to train with: Lecoq, complicite, The School for Wise Children, Frantic Assembly, and Gecko.

Delyth Evans | Set and Costume Designer

Forthcoming credits include: *Mavra and Pierrot Lunaire* (Royal Opera House, Covent Garden); *Gulliver's Travels* (Unicorn Theatre); *The Two Character Play* (Hampstead Theatre, Upstairs); *Glass Menagerie* (Royal Exchange, Manchester); *Cat on a Hot Tin Roof* (Curve Theatre and UK Tour), *The Enemy* (Royal National Theatre of Scotland).

Theatre credits include: *Harm* (Bush Theatre); *The Comeback* (Sonia Friedman Productions, Noel Coward theatre – West End); *Harm Film* (BBC Films); *Incantata* (Irish Rep Theatre,

NYC); *Hedda Gabler* (Sherman Theatre); *The Phlebotomist* (Hampstead Theatre); *Midsummer Party* (The Old Vic); *The Audience* (Nuffield Theatre); *Don Carlos* (Exeter Northcott); *Incantata* (Galway Festival); *An Adventure, Leave Taking* (The Bush Theatre); *Yous Two* (Hampstead Theatre); *The Almighty Sometimes* (Royal Exchange Theatre); *King Lear* (Globe Theatre); *Earthworks and Myth* (RSC); *Low Level Panic* (Orange Tree Theatre); *After October* (Finborough Theatre); *Henry I* (Reading Between the Lines); *Girls* (Soho Theatre, Hightide & Talawa Theatre); *Fup and Noye's Fludde* (Kneehigh Theatre); *Dark Land Lighthouse* (Bristol Old Vic); *St Joan of the Stockyards*; *A Thousand Seasons Passed*; *The Tinder Box*; *The Last Days of Mankind*; TALON (Bristol Old Vic); *Diary of a Madman*; *The Rise and Shine of Comrade Fiasco* (The Gate Theatre); *Infinite Lives*; *Coastal Defences* (Tobacco Factory Theatre); *Banksy: The Room in the Elephant* (Tobacco Factory Theatre and Traverse Theatre).

Danny Vavrečka | Lighting Designer

Danny is a lighting designer based in London. Theatre includes: *work.txt* (Soho Theatre); *Period Dramas* (Other Palace Studio); *Jigsaw* (Rose Theatre); *The Moors* (Richard Burton Theatre); *Fires Our Shoes Have Made* (Edinburgh Fringe); *X* (Warwick Arts Centre Studio); *Blood Wedding* (Mumford Theatre). Musical Theatre includes: *Dogfight* (Warwick Arts Centre Studio); *Timpson: The Musical* (King's Head Theatre); *RENT* (Goose Nest Theatre); *Guys and Dolls* (Warwick Arts Centre Theatre).

Dance includes: *Terra Nova* (Theatre Royal Winchester); *1001* (Omnibus Theatre). Opera includes: *Beauty and the Seven Beasts* (Brixton Jamm); *Don Giovanni / Il barbiere di Siviglia / Le nozze di Figaro* (Sherman Theatre); *Hansel and*

Gretel (Goose Nest Theatre). Danny trained at the Royal Welsh College of Music & Drama, following a degree in Theatre at the University of Warwick.

Hattie North | Sound Designer

Hattie North is a Sound Designer from Leeds, now based in London. Her work includes *Shake The City* (Leeds Playhouse); *Princess Essex* (Mercury Theatre) and *The Borrowers* (Theatre By The Lake).

Misha Mah | Production Manager

Misha Mah is a Production Manager, currently based in London. Theatre credits include: *Zombiegate* (Theatre503); *A Gig For Ghosts* (Soho Theatre); *CASTE-ING*, *Hungry* (Paines Plough, Roundabout), *Kabul Goes Pop: Music Television Afghanistan* (Brixton House & Touring); *Til Death Do Us Part* (Theatre503).

Nikita Bala | Stage Manager

Nikita Bala is a Stage Manager and Technician with a passion for anything going on backstage. She has worked in Montreal, Toronto, Malmo, Dusseldorf, and Bangalore, and is excited to now call London home. She is the 2019 recipient of the Montreal English Theatre Award for Outstanding Emerging Artist (Production).

About AHP

Ameena Hamid Productions is a leading London based theatrical production company working across the commercial and subsidised sectors. We specialise in creative theatre production, podcast production, general management, and research and development.

AHP works almost exclusively in new work (both plays and musicals) and strives to create brilliant work that feels both timely and timeless putting inclusivity and representation at the heart of what we do. The company is led by Ameena Hamid, a powerhouse producer and general manager.

Ameena has been heralded as "a true role model to the future generations" by Official London Theatre and was one of The Stage 25, a list of twenty five theatremakers to watch out for in 2022 and beyond. She holds the title of youngest producer on the West End having cut her teeth as Associate Producer on Death Drop. She was Theatre Producer at Soho Theatre and is on the Board of the League of Independent Producers and was part of the Creative Freelances Shaping London's Recovery Advisory Group 2021.

AHP was the General Manager on Wonderville Magic and Illusion, and Co-Producer on the critically acclaimed The Wiz with Hope Mill Theatre Manchester. Other credits include: Co-Producer in Dick Whittington (Phoenix Theatre), Producer on Graduates at Cadogan Hall (Streamed Digitally), Assistant Producer on The Show Must Go On Live (Palace Theatre), Producer on Eating Myself (Applecart Arts and FAE Lima, Peru), Producer on Killing It and Since U Been Gone (VAULT Festival).

Theatre503 is at the forefront of identifying and nurturing new voices at the very start of their careers and launching them into the industry. They stage more early career playwrights than any other theatre in the world – with over 120 writers premiered each year from festivals of short pieces to full length productions, resulting in employment for over 1,000 freelance artists through their year-round programme.

Theatre503 provides a diverse pipeline of talent resulting in modern classics like **The Mountaintop** by Katori Hall and **Rotterdam** by Jon Brittain – both Olivier Award winners – to future classics like Yasmin Joseph's **J'Ouvert**, winner of the 2020 James Tait Black Prize and transferred to the West End/BBC Arts and **Wolfie** by Ross Willis, winner of the 2020 Writers Guild Award for Best New Play. Writers who began their creative life at Theatre503 are now writing for the likes of *The Crown, Succession, Doctor Who, Killing Eve* and *Normal People* and every single major subsidised theatre in the country now boasts a new play by a writer who started at Theatre503.

THEATRE503 TEAM

Artistic Director	Lisa Spirling
Executive Director	Andrew Shepherd
Literary Manager	Steve Harper
Producer	Ceri Lothian
General Manager	Tash Berg
Carne Associate Director	Jade Lewis
Literary Associate	Lauretta Barrow
Trainee Assistant Producers	Catherine Moriarty, Tsipora St. Clair Knights

Our Supporters

We are particularly grateful to Philip and Christine Carne and the long term support of The Carne Trust for our International Playwriting Award, the 503Five and Carne Associate.

Share The Drama Patrons: *Angela Hyde-Courtney, Eilene Davidson, Cas & Philip Donald, Erica Whyman, Geraldine Sharpe-Newton, Jack Tilbury/Plann, Jennifer Jacobs, Jill Segal, Joachim Fleury, Jon and NoraLee Sedmak, Ali Taylor, Tim Roseman, Berlin Associates, DavidsonMorris Solicitors, Eric Bensaude, Ian Mill KC, Jenny Sheridan, Liberty Oberlander, Marcus Markou & Dynamis, Marianne Badrichani, Mike Morfey, Nick Hern, Pam Alexander & Roger Booker, Patricia Hamzahee, Richard Bean, Robert O'Dowd, Tom Gowans, Tim Willcox, The Bell Family, Sean Winnett* and all our 503 Friends and Share The Drama supporters.

The Foyle Foundation, Arts Council England Grants for the Arts, Garrick Charitable Trust, Cockayne Grants for the Arts (503 Productions), Noel Coward Foundation (Rapid Write Response) The Orseis Trust (503Five), Battersea Power Station Foundation (Right to Write), Wimbledon Foundation (Five-O-Fresh), Concord Theatricals (503 International Playwriting Award), Wandsworth Borough Council, The Theatres Trust.

With Thanks

Making theatre is hard, trying to make theatre during a pandemic is even harder. I've been working on *Zombiegate* for many years and to be honest there have been many times when I thought it would not see the light of day. Given its long journey from page to stage there are a lot of people I need to thank.

Thank you, Lisa Spirling, Steve Harper, Andrew Shepherd and all the staff at Theatre503 for programming the play and supporting the production. Thank you to our incredible creative team Aled, Danny, Delyth, Hattie, Misha, Nikita and Phoebe. Our wonderful cast Chand, Ebony, George and Virginia for bringing the ideas and characters I've had running around my head for years to life.

Thank you to Fraser Grace for your mentorship and for first suggesting that you could see this play finding a home at 503. Thank you to Hazel Kerr and everyone at Masterclass TRH and the staff of Theatre Royal Haymarket for supporting the rehearsed reading of the play back in 2018. Thank you to Luke Roebuck, Anton Lesser, Sir Derek Jacobi and Sir David Hare.

Thank you to the incredible Ameena Hamid for your wisdom and talent, thank you to Julian Bruton for all your passionate work and support and believing in the play even when I did not. Thank you to my parents, family and friends who have supported me over the years and a huge thank you to Oonagh for always believing in me.

Finally, a huge thank you to our audience for taking a chance on a piece of new writing, live theatre is one of the oldest artforms we need to support and protect all parts of the industry if it is to thrive.   **M.G.**

Characters

SOPHIE

JAMIE

SIMON

DANIELLE

MARCIA

JENNIFER

CHUCK

TONY

Puppets

TOWN CRIER

PUNCH

JUDY

BABY

CLOWN

DEVIL

POLICEMAN

CROCODILE

Note on the space: On the stage as the audience enter is a Punch and Judy Theatre booth with red and white stripes. A sign hangs from it reading "the next trolling will begin at" and a clock face set for the time the performance is due to start. The Punch and Judy Theatre remains on stage throughout.

ONE

Sophie and Jamie are waiting at a bus stop dressed as zombies.

SOPHIE: Come on, let's take a selfie.

JAMIE: What for?

SOPHIE: Instagram. Come on it will be fun. Hashtag Zombie Selfie.

JAMIE: Do we have to?

SOPHIE: Please?

JAMIE: You know I hate having my photo taken.

SOPHIE: I've spent all afternoon on that costume, let me show it off. One photo?

JAMIE: Fine.

Sophie pulls out her phone, Jamie stands next to her.

You need to get closer to me.

SOPHIE: Kneel down you're too tall.

JAMIE: If you hold it like that, you'll get glare from the streetlights.

SOPHIE: Ow! Watch my feet.

JAMIE: Soz. Lift it up more. Higher.

SOPHIE: For someone who hates them, you sure do know a lot.

JAMIE: Look if you're going to do it. Do it right.

SOPHIE: How's that?

JAMIE: Perfect.

SOPHIE: Great say cheese.

                 No, let's do zombie faces.

They pull zombie faces. Sophie takes the photo.

                 What do you think?

JAMIE: Cool.

SOPHIE: Does it need a filter?

JAMIE: Nah, that's a no filter job.

Sophie loads the photo to Instagram.

                 Look let's just sack tonight off. By the time
                 we get there the party will be over. How
                 about we stay in with a horror film and
                 Maccies?

SOPHIE: I have spent enough time in that flat to last
                 me a lifetime. I am going out tonight, Jamie,
                 I'm going to Molly's Halloween Party, I am
                 going to get drunk, and I am going to dance.

JAMIE: You can get drunk and make a fool of
                 yourself back at the flat.

SOPHIE: Why are you going to dance with me?

JAMIE: I'm not a dancer.

SOPHIE: Oh, come on.

Sophie attempts to dance with Jamie.

JAMIE: No, get off. I think the bus is coming.

The bus doesn't come.

Jamie picks his make-up.

SOPHIE: Don't you dare start picking at your make-up! It took ages.

JAMIE: I wasn't.

He picks it again

SOPHIE: I saw that.

JAMIE: I wasn't picking, I was scratching.

SOPHIE: Well don't.

Jamie goes to pick again

Will you leave it, God I feel sorry for the poor woman who ends up with you. You never listen.

JAMIE: It's itchy.

SOPHIE: It's expensive.

JAMIE: I think I might be allergic.

SOPHIE: Well, you should have thought about that before you made me buy the expensive make-up.

JAMIE: I didn't make you / buy expensive.

SOPHIE: "I'm only coming if we can go as zombies."

JAMIE: I only said that because you won't let me wear my usual costume.

SOPHIE: Wearing a t-shirt that says life and handing out lemons isn't a proper Halloween costume.

JAMIE: When life gives you lemons.

SOPHIE: Yeah, I get it.

Sophie looks at her phone.

Nobody liked our photo.

JAMIE: No, no. Don't be that person. You only posted it a minute ago, already you're checking your phone to see how popular you are.

SOPHIE: Sorry.

JAMIE: See that's the problem with social media, everyone desperately posting everything that happens to them in the vain hope that it will attract likes.

SOPHIE: I just want people to know what I'm doing. I look at friends from school and they're getting married or having babies. I just want to show them that I'm doing something with my life.

JAMIE: Why do you care? Besides. It's all bollocks. Nobody's Instagram is a true reflection of their life. People only share the best bits. Holiday photos, weddings. Nobody ever posts photos of them in their pants, at three o'clock on a Sunday afternoon, watching Netflix. It's really sad actually people pretending to be something they're not just to impress a bunch of algorithms.

SOPHIE: Well, I'm sorry for wanting a photo of the two of us.

Jamie gets down on one knee.

JAMIE: I'm sorry. Will you marry me? Well, it would make for a good Instagram story.

SOPHIE: You're a dick.

JAMIE: Perhaps, but if any of your single mates ask after me, I'd prefer it if you used words like "mysterious" and "aloof".

SOPHIE: I see, how about "pretentious" and "a bit of a twat".

Sophie checks her phone.

JAMIE: Any exciting updates?

SOPHIE: Look, if I want to get work at one of the bigger charities, then I need to have a bigger social media following. Some charity comms people have thousands of followers, I only have 748.

JAMIE: It's really sad you know how many followers you have.

SOPHIE: Like you're any better.

JAMIE: I am actually.

SOPHIE: You're constantly on Twitter.

JAMIE: Twitter is different.

SOPHIE: How is it different?

JAMIE: Two words. Elon Musk.

SOPHIE: He's such a dick.

JAMIE: Nah, he's laugh.

SOPHIE: A laugh? He's a billionaire Jamie, not your mate. It obvious by the way the whole I don't care what people think of me, is an act. Deep down you're as desperate as everyone else to be liked.

JAMIE: I only use Twitter for professional reasons. If you want to make it as a journalist these days, you have to be on Twitter.

SOPHIE: If you want to make it as a journalist *these days*. You need to actually do some writing.

JAMIE: I write, I make memes.

SOPHIE: Can you call making memes journalism?

JAMIE: You sound like my Dad.

SOPHIE:	Well, maybe he's got a point.
JAMIE:	It's not my fault I've got no work. I'm waiting on him to speak to his mate from the club about that internship.
SOPHIE:	Do you ever think about getting married?
JAMIE:	To you?
SOPHIE:	No, obviously, I mean in general.
JAMIE:	Nah, not really…hardly…occasionally.
SOPHIE:	Cool…
JAMIE:	How's your Mum?

Sophie sighs.

SOPHIE:	Do you actually want to know how my Mum is or is this a set up for one of your 'jokes'?
JAMIE:	I genuinely want to know. How is Jennifer?
SOPHIE:	Ridiculous, ever since she moved to that village. She's become so twee. She joined the school board of governors and the May Day Committee, she never use to do anything like that when I was a kid. Next thing you know she'll be making her own jam.
JAMIE:	Ah first it's jam, then it becomes knitwear before you know where you they're imprisoning outsiders in a wicker man and setting fire to them.

SOPHIE: She's moved to the countryside, not joined a cult.

JAMIE: Same thing.

SOPHIE: Your parents live in the countryside.

JAMIE: Exactly.

Sophie checks her phone

You're so addicted to your phone.

SOPHIE: You're just as bad. I bet I could go longer without my phone than you.

JAMIE: No, you couldn't.

SOPHIE: I could go all night without my phone.

JAMIE: I'd like to see you try, you're a social media junkie.

SOPHIE: Oh and you're not?

JAMIE: I'd last longer than you.

SOPHIE: Is that what you say to all the girls?

JAMIE: I'm serious I could go all night without my phone.

SOPHIE: Wanna bet?

JAMIE: Yeah, alright. I bet a week's worth of washing up, I can go all night without my phone, and you can't.

SOPHIE: Two weeks.

JAMIE: Deal.

They shake on it, get out their phones turn them off. Sound of a bus approaching.

Light fades.

A montage of social media notifications and vibrations.

TWO

Lights up on Punch & Judy Theatre Booth.

Town Crier enters ringing a bell.

TOWN C: Oyez, Oyez, Oyez! All good citizens draw near,

Be you a punter from Covent Garden or Brighton Pier,

For 360 years our little puppet show would entertain,

On windy beaches and village fêtes in the baking sun and pouring rain,

The tragical comedy or is it comical tragedy of Mr Punch?

Once regarded as a timeless fable, now declared out of touch,

We were told the dark humour must be replaced,

With family friendly pantomime to stay on the right side of good taste,

Or we must find a new domain where nobody would get upset,

A space where manners are not needed, a place we call the internet.

Town Crier exits. Mr Punch enters.

23

PUNCH: Hollo, Boyz and Girlz it's me Mr Punch! Oh, dear you're a horrible looking lot. I'll suppose you'll have to do. Now I've got some lovely sausages, but the crocodile is jealous because he's a millennial and he's spent all his money on avocados and flat whites. Now he's trying to steal my sausages.

Phone notification.

Oi! You're in a theatre, phones should be switch... Oh hang on it's mine.

Punch exits returns with phone.

What's going on here? Zombie selfie, but they're... that's not good. Well well would you look at this. 2 people dressed as Zombies mocking a floral tribute to a dead child. One of them works for the charity Wishing Well for terminally ill children. Well, we can't have that can we Boyz and Girlz? Think I'll give them a piece of my mind.

Punch begins to send message.

"Disgusting behaviour she'll need more than Halloween make-up when I'm finished with her." "If somebody works with Sophie Cooper do me a favour and rape her in her lunch break." Haha that's the way to do it.

Lights fade on Booth.

THREE

Sophie and Jamie's flat the next morning, the kitchen/living room. Sophie is in a dressing gown, Jamie enters hungover.

SOPHIE:	Morning.
JAMIE:	I want to die.
SOPHIE:	Hung over?
JAMIE:	No. Maybe a little.

Beat

Oh God. Why did you let me drink gin?

SOPHIE:	Couldn't really stop you. Brew?
JAMIE:	Yes please.

Sophie begins to make tea.

SOPHIE:	So, admit it, you had fun last night?
JAMIE:	Dunno, can't really remember, I had gin.
SOPHIE:	Gin is fun.
JAMIE:	Every atom of my body currently disagrees with you.
SOPHIE:	If you're this hungover in the morning, it because you had fun the night before.
JAMIE:	If I admit I had fun will you be quiet?
SOPHIE:	Maybe.

JAMIE: I had fun.

SOPHIE: Yay!

JAMIE: Ssshh noises.

SOPHIE: Sorry.

JAMIE: I didn't do anything embarrassing last night?

Beat

          Soph?

SOPHIE: No… You're a good dancer.

Jamie collapses with embarrassment.

          It wasn't that bad; you've got some real moves.

JAMIE: Did we dance?

SOPHIE: Hell yeah!

JAMIE: Oh shit! Now I remember.

SOPHIE: *(sings)* I said, certified freak. Seven days a week, wet-ass…

JAMIE: Don't!

SOPHIE: Think you know a guy and then you find out he can twerk. You were on fire.

JAMIE: We both were.

SOPHIE: True. We were hot.

JAMIE: We were dressed as rotting undead corpses.

SOPHIE: Thank you.

JAMIE: What for?

SOPHIE: Coming out with me, it really meant a lot.

JAMIE: No problem, I'm glad I listened to you, I had a great time, I think. It was nice to have some fun.

SOPHIE: Good to get out of the flat! Be with other people.

JAMIE: Yeah, be with other people but also together.

SOPHIE: Yeah. Oh, you've got...some make up still on your face.

JAMIE: Oh, have I got it?

SOPHIE: No.

JAMIE: Here.

SOPHIE: No. It's more. Let me.

Sophie rubs the make-up off Jamie's face. They share a moment.

JAMIE: And neither of us checked our phones all night.

SOPHIE: Oh my god my phone is still off. Where is it? Must have left it in my room.

Sophie exits

Jamie anxiously paces

Sophie re-enters carrying her phone

JAMIE: Soph, there's something / I need to tell you.

SOPHIE: Fuck. Jamie. Fuck. Look at this.

JAMIE: What?

SOPHIE: It's the selfie.

JAMIE: What?

SOPHIE: Look. In the background.

Jamie takes the phone he looks.

JAMIE: Oh shit.

SOPHIE: Read the comments.

JAMIE: Wait they don't think we did that on purpose?

SOPHIE: Yeah.

JAMIE: Shit, how have people seen this?

SOPHIE: It's gone viral.

JAMIE: But your account is private.

SOPHIE: No.

JAMIE: What?

SOPHIE: You get more followers if it's public. Look what we've done.

JAMIE:	I mean obviously, we're not doing what they think we're doing.
SOPHIE:	I've got missed calls from my Mum, you don't think she's seen it?
JAMIE:	How?
SOPHIE:	It's been on the news.
JAMIE:	What? Hang on where's my phone.
SOPHIE:	Have your parents said anything?
JAMIE:	I can't find my phone.
SOPHIE:	Listen to this "The Zombie selfie dubbed by many as Zombiegate first went viral on Saturday night after an image and link to Sophie Cooper's Instagram was shared across multiple social media platforms." We should say sorry.
JAMIE:	No.
SOPHIE:	We need to say sorry now.
JAMIE:	Just wait, let me find my phone.
SOPHIE:	We've made fun of a dead child.
JAMIE:	No. We. Haven't. We took a photo of ourselves.
SOPHIE:	Dressed as /Zombies.
JAMIE:	On Halloween.

SOPHIE: In front of a floral tribute to a dead child.

JAMIE: We didn't see that.

SOPHIE: A floral tribute to a kid who was killed last week.

JAMIE: We didn't see it.

SOPHIE: I feel sick.

JAMIE: Soph, listen to me, we haven't done anything wrong. People are just overreacting.

Jamie hunts for his phone

SOPHIE: We've offended people.

JAMIE: Not on purpose. You can't give offence. You can only take it. They're only…

SOPHIE: People are really aggressive online.

JAMIE: Just block them. Set your account to private.

SOPHIE: Fuck.

JAMIE: What?

SOPHIE: Look at this one from @Mr_Punch.

She hands him the phone; he barely looks at the message.

JAMIE: They're just trying to upset you.

SOPHIE: Well, it's working. I'm going to say something.

JAMIE:	Don't say anything until I've spoken to my Dad.
SOPHIE:	Call your Dad? This isn't your share of the electricity bill. You can't make this go away with a magical wave of your parents' credit card.
JAMIE:	What is that supposed to mean?
SOPHIE:	Nothing. I'm saying sorry. I'm going to write an apology.
JAMIE:	Saying sorry is a sign of weakness.
SOPHIE:	People are reasonable. Once we explain.
JAMIE:	Reasonable? Have you been on the internet?

Jamie spots his phone.

It's here.

Picks it up and turns it on.

SOPHIE:	Well, what should we do then?
JAMIE:	Make your account private.
SOPHIE:	But if I make it private people won't see the apology.
JAMIE:	Good, you shouldn't be saying sorry.
SOPHIE:	We have to say something.
JAMIE:	No, you don't. You see these things all the time. It's like in Frankenstein, the villagers,

are just looking for an excuse to burn down the windmill. They blame the creature because he's in the wrong place at the wrong time.

SOPHIE: This isn't some horror film Jamie.

JAMIE: People are just looking for drama. Next week someone else will break ranks and they'll chase them.

SOPHIE: Look at this, people signing a petition to get me fired.

JAMIE: You're not going to get fired for taking a selfie.

SOPHIE: We can't just ignore this. It's too big. I'm writing an apology.

Sophie gets out her phone begins to type.

Hello, please share this with everyone you know. I want this to be seen by as many people as possible. Last night myself and my friend Jamie.

JAMIE: Don't include me.

SOPHIE: Jamie?

JAMIE: I'm serious.

SOPHIE: Fine.

I took a photo of myself dressed as a zombie whilst at a bus stop waiting to go to a fancy dress party. I am so sorry for any offence caused. I did not mean to upset anyone. It was dark, I didn't see the flowers. I am deeply sorry for offence caused, especially to the family and friends.

JAMIE: Write it in notes and then / save it.

SOPHIE: Of that young boy and I mean it from the bottom of my heart. I hope this clears up the matter. Yours Sophie Cooper.

JAMIE: OK save it.

Sophie uploads it.

SOPHIE: This is the right thing to do. How many times have your parents called?

JAMIE: They haven't.

SOPHIE: That's good that means they haven't seen it?

JAMIE: I think you just made a terrible mistake.

Jamie exits.

Blackout.

FOUR

Lights up on Punch and Judy Booth. Clown & Punch

PUNCH: Hello Joey the Clown.

CLOWN: Hello Mr Punch what have you been up to?

PUNCH: I've been having a great time trolling those 2 disgusting fuckwits from the Zombiegate selfie *(laughs)*.

CLOWN: You're the best at the trolling, I wish I could troll like you.

PUNCH: Trolling not that hard there's just a few simple rules would you like hear them?

CLOWN: Yes please.

PUNCH: Rule one. Choose your target – the secret to a good trolling is to find the right target, someone who deserves it, someone who stepped out of line. Someone awful.

CLOWN: Like that bitch from the Zombiegate selfie?

PUNCH: Exactly! Rule two, don't get banned. You're going to piss people off so make sure you've got lots of different accounts you can switch to. Rule three, know your memes, keep it funny keep it fresh. Trolling is all about having fun! Rule four, when in doubt saying the worst thing imaginable, if you can't be witty or clever be outrageous, the more extreme the better.

CLOWN: I'm not very good at being outrageous.

PUNCH: Ah that's the easy part. Take Zombiegate for instance, I was starting to run out of ideas so I just thought of the most disgusting thing I could and ended up sending her this. "If someone works with Sophie Copper do me a favour and rape her in her lunch break."

Clown laughs

CLOWN: That's really funny.

PUNCH: Thanks man, that's the thing to remember we're doing this for the lolz.

Lights fade on booth

FIVE

Sophie's workplace the next day. Sophie sits at a table with Simon and Danielle on the other side.

SOPHIE: You're firing me?

DANIELLE: We're letting you go.

SIMON: I'm very sorry Sophie but the truth of the matter is, you continuing to work for us, it's become, it's become untenable.

DANIELLE: There is an overwhelming amount of public pressure on Wishing Well, at this time. The charity sector as I'm sure you're aware is under a lot of scrutiny, we exist entirely on public donations, our continuation depends on people's good will.

SOPHIE: Perhaps if you let me draft a statement?

DANIELLE: I don't think that would be wise, there's already an electronic petition. Do you know what that is?

SOPHIE: I know what an e-petition is! Simon, please you can't do this.

SIMON: I'm sorry, that petition has thousands of signatures. Wishing Well has a reputation to maintain.

DANIELLE: Currently it's close to seven thousand and rising.

SOPHIE:	Please, give me another chance, it's just some silly.
SIMON:	The Board are getting very nervous.
DANIELLE:	We've had people cancelling their direct debts all morning.
SIMON:	I'm sorry Sophie there's nothing I can do.
SOPHIE:	I don't understand I said sorry, look. I thought if I explained myself, it would make things better.

Danielle takes Sophie's phone and reads the apology.

DANIELLE:	"I am sorry for any offence caused; I didn't see the flowers" You didn't see the flowers? They're a bit hard to miss on the photo.
SOPHIE:	I wasn't looking at the background I was looking…
DANIELLE:	At yourself?
SOPHIE:	I uploaded it in a hurry.
SIMON:	Come on Sophie, you work in communications, you know, you continuing to work with us is not possible. I'll give you a fantastic reference.
SOPHIE:	This can't be legal.
DANIELLE:	This action is in keeping with our social media policy. Details of our social media policy, can be found in our employee

	handbook, I presume you have read the employee handbook? If you like I can send a copy to your union rep?
SOPHIE:	I'm not in the union.
DANIELLE:	Oh, well never mind.
SIMON:	I'll need your key card. Danielle will show you out. If you have any personal belongings / we can get these.
SOPHIE:	Simon you can't do this to me.
SIMON:	Come on Sophie! We're a charity for terminally ill children, we can't employ someone who takes photos of themselves mocking dead kids.
SOPHIE:	That wasn't what I was doing, it was just a stupid selfie.
SIMON:	We require good will from people.
SOPHIE:	This will blow over, next week they'll be angry at someone else.
SIMON:	Not whilst you work here. I mean if you can't / see that.
DANIELLE:	I think what Simon is trying to say.
SOPHIE:	Do you know how much fucking shit I've been through?
DANIELLE:	Please don't swear.

SOPHIE: For the last twenty-four hours all I've got is abuse, people threating to rape me, kill me. I mean how can someone be offended by me supposedly mocking the dead and then say stuff like "I want to fuck you with a broken bottle"?

SIMON: We know this is a difficult time for you, and the charity is grateful, I am grateful for your service, if you need to speak to someone, I'm sure, Danielle will only be too happy to help.

DANIELLE: Sure, anything you need.

SOPHIE: Look at this, one guy on twitter, called Mr. Punch, over a hundred messages from him, each one more vulgar than the next. I blocked him, fifteen minutes later, he's sending me abuse from another account, Mr. Punch 95.

SIMON: Obviously we don't approve.

SOPHIE: look at what the people signing your petition are saying.

DANIELLE: It's not our petition.

SOPHIE: Look at it.

SIMON: I don't need to see it.

SOPHIE: You don't need to see it? You don't need to see? This is what I have to put up with for the last two days! It's sick and you're giving

into them, you're throwing me under the
bus.

SIMON: You should have /thought.

SOPHIE: I mean if you give into them how are you
any better?

SIMON: You should have thought about that before
you sent the photo.

DANIELLE: Sophie, we don't condone the abuse, we want
to support you, really we do, but you can't
keep your job here. We're very sorry.

Blackout

SIX

Lights up on Punch and Judy Booth, Judy enters

JUDY: Mr Punch, Mr Punch!

Punch appears

PUNCH: Hollo.

JUDY: I'm going shopping and I need you to look after the baby.

PUNCH: Baby! When did we get a baby?

JUDY: We've always had a baby.

Judy exits and re-enters holding the baby

PUNCH: What if it cries?

JUDY: Sing him a lullaby.

Judy exits

PUNCH: Look after the baby Punch, unbelievable, Cultural Marxism that what this is!

Baby cries

Oh no the baby's crying. I'll sing it a lullaby. Bah Bah black sheep have you any wool, yes sir, yes sir, three bags full.

Baby cries

Oh, you don't like that bloody snowflake. Howz about Jack and Jill went up the hill, to fetch a pail of water, Jack fell down and

41

broke his crown, and Jill came tumbling after.

Baby cries

Libtard!

Hits the baby against the side of the stage

Oh, you filthy baby! What have you done?

Hit the baby's head several times against the side of the stage.

The baby stops crying.

There, there little one, that's the way to do it.

JUDY: Hello, I'm back with the shopping.

PUNCH: That was quick!

Judy enters

JUDY: Where's the baby?

PUNCH: The baby? What baby?

JUDY: Our baby.

PUNCH: He's left home.

JUDY: Left home? I've only been gone a minute.

Sophie enters the space watching from a distance.

PUNCH: They grow up so fast these days.

Judy looks down

JUDY: Oh my god, the baby!

Judy exits re-enters with a slapstick and hits Punch, they fight. Punch gets hold of the slapstick and hits Judy repeatedly until she collapses.

PUNCH: That's the way to...

SOPHIE: Are you the Mr Punch who's been trolling me?

PUNCH: I'm the Lord of Misrule, I'm here there and everywhere. Who the fuck are you?

SOPHIE: Zombiegate.

Punch laughs

                    So, that's a yes?

PUNCH: Hard to say, I'm a busy guy.

SOPHIE: Busy beating up women and children?

Judy gets back up

JUDY: It's called a joke sweetheart, look it up.

SOPHIE: Is saying I should be raped a joke?

PUNCH: Raping you would be pretty funny.

Punch and Judy laugh.

JUDY: Sticks and stones may break my bones but words will never hurt me.

SOPHIE: That's your defense for the things you say.

PUNCH:	You're the one who's been mocking dead children.
SOPHIE:	That's not what happened, we didn't see.
PUNCH:	Didn't see, didn't see. To busy looking at your ugly fat face.
SOPHIE:	I lost my job because of people like you.
PUNCH:	No, you lost it because of your own behaviour.
SOPHIE:	Even if I did do what you think, do you really believe being fired is a fair punishment?
PUNCH:	I'm sure your rich Mummy and Daddy will look after you.
SOPHIE:	Hardly rich, Mum is doing Ok for herself now, but it hasn't been easy.
PUNCH:	Hashtag first world problems.
SOPHIE:	I'm not a bad person, I worked for a charity.
PUNCH:	Wishing Well?
SOPHIE:	Yeah.
PUNCH:	Just think of all those families at their most vulnerable putting their faith and trust in that charity. Imagine how they felt when they saw that selfie, when they discovered they'd been supporting the like of you. They must have felt sick.

SOPHIE: But I've been fired now, and yet you still send me abuse. When is this going to stop.

PUNCH: When you learnt your lesson.

SOPHIE: What sort of lesson is photoshopping my face onto a dead woman's body meant to teach me?

JUDY: Wait he did what?

PUNCH: Consequences.

SOPHIE: Consequences?

JUDY: Consequences?

PUNCH: Consequences.

SOPHIE: The abuse you send is a million times worse than anything I ever did.

PUNCH: Or maybe I'm just doing it for the lolz *(laughs)*.

SOPHIE: Surely, you must get tired of this. He gets to dish out abuse, beat you and the baby. Where are the consequences for his actions? It's one rule for Punch another for everyone else.

PUNCH: That's because I'm the Lord of Misrule, an agent of chaos, Old Red Nose himself.

SOPHIE: Who are you really? Behind the avatar, who is pulling the strings?

PUNCH: I'm a glove puppet.

SOPHIE: You're hiding yourself because you know what you're doing is wrong.

PUNCH: This isn't your world it's mine. There are different rules here. You broke the rules and now you must be punished.

SOPHIE: Me and Jamie don't deserve this we're good people.

PUNCH: You think he's a good person? *(laughs)*

SOPHIE: What's funny about that?

PUNCH: Your friend is a racist.

SOPHIE: No, he's not.

PUNCH: Ask him what he use to tweet about when he was 17, because I know. Go have a look for yourself. See the jokes he used to make. I know who he really is and soon so will everybody else. This isn't the end; it's only just beginning. That's the way to do it.

Sophie exits.

JUDY: Actually, she's got a point. It's one rule for you another for the rest of us. You bludgeoned your way through life and if anyone criticises, you say it's only a joke. Well, I don't find it funny, not anymore things need to change around here.

Judy exits.

PUNCH: Ok boyz and girlz you all saw what happened there. I was attacked by a group of extremists. Feminazis trying to cancel my free speech. Did you know fifty percent of all domestic abuse cases are carried out by women? Just because that's a fact I made up doesn't mean it's not true.

Lights fade on Booth.

SEVEN

Sophie and Jamie's Flat, a suitcase half packed and open in the centre Jamie enters on the phone.

JAMIE: No, no I understand, not his fault. Yeah, bad timing. To be honest these things happen like all the time, and I reckon in a couple of months everyone would have forgotten this. So, I was thinking maybe they could take me on in like 6 months' time? Or I could write an article about the new McCarthyism the reality of social media. I know you're busy, no. I am grateful, well maybe pass on his email to me and I can contact him. Fine, fine, no it was just an idea.

Spots suitcase

Sorry Dad, I've got to go, send my love to Mum, no, no. Fine I'll call later. Bye.

Sophie enters carrying a handful of clothes, starts to pack them into the suitcase.

JAMIE: What's with the suitcase?

SOPHIE: Packing.

JAMIE: Why?

SOPHIE: I can't stay here.

JAMIE: You'll get another job.

SOPHIE: They put where we live online.

JAMIE:	You don't seriously think? Relax. The police said if we see anything suspicious, we were to call them.
SOPHIE:	There's people online saying there going to come to my flat and rape me.

Sophie exits

Sophie re-enters with more clothes

JAMIE:	We're safe here, I can keep us safe. I double check the doors are locked every night.
SOPHIE:	You just don't get it do you?
JAMIE:	Where are you going to go?
SOPHIE:	My Mum's.
JAMIE:	That's nowhere near here.
SOPHIE:	I know.
JAMIE:	What about this place?
SOPHIE:	My Mum's agreed to pay the rent for the next month, so you've got time to find a new flatmate.
JAMIE:	New flatmate? Shouldn't we talk about this?
SOPHIE:	I can't stay here; I need time away from everything.
JAMIE:	That's bullshit.
SOPHIE:	Can you let me pass?

JAMIE: No.

SOPHIE: Please Jamie. I've already booked the train, I'm going tonight.

JAMIE: Tonight? Why didn't you discuss this with me?

SOPHIE: Because it's none of your business. / Now let me pass

JAMIE: Yes it is. That selfie is of both of us, we're in this together.

SOPHIE: No, we're not. You haven't been fired.

JAMIE: You'll get another job. This is all going to blow over.

SOPHIE: I don't want to talk about this. Now move.

Sophie forces herself past Jamie and exits.

Sophie re-enters with more things to pack

JAMIE: Why are you running away?

SOPHIE: I'm not running away. Mum thinks a change of scenery will do me good. Maybe you should do the same go and see your parents?

JAMIE: There's really no need for this, I'm telling you another 48 hours and everyone would have forgotten this ever even happened.

SOPHIE: Do you remember what type of things you used to tweet as a teenager?

JAMIE: What?

SOPHIE: I found some old tweets of yours, they're really horrible.

JAMIE: Like what?

SOPHIE: Dead baby jokes.

JAMIE: I don't think I did.

SOPHIE: "What do you call a dead baby in a blender?"

JAMIE: I was just trying to be provocative, shocking, get a reaction. All kids did it. How did you even find them?

SOPHIE: I confronted one of the trolls, asked him why he was attacking me.

JAMIE: Christ Soph, why the hell would you do that? That's what they want attention. Fat sweaty losers with nothing else going on in their lives. Saying the worst thing they can think of so people will notice them.

SOPHIE: He calls himself Mr Punch. He's written some horrible things about me.

JAMIE: Just block him!

SOPHIE: What's the point? He just sets up a new account. Trolls like that are always one step ahead. He's smart like that.

JAMIE: If he is a he.

SOPHIE: Of course, he's a he. He told me about your old tweets.

JAMIE: Everyone wrote stupid stuff when they were a teenager.

SOPHIE: They're going to publish them. They're going to expose you as a racist.

JAMIE: What the? / I'm not.

SOPHIE: "How many police does it take to push a black man down some stairs? None he fell".

JAMIE: That is obviously a satirical joke about police brutality.

SOPHIE: "How do you kill a hundred Mexicans? Blow up their van." I'm not repeating the rest.

JAMIE: I was a stupid kid.

SOPHIE: I can't believe I live with someone who thinks like this.

JAMIE: I don't think that. They're clearly jokes.

SOPHIE: That's just what Mr Punch says about what he writes. They're just jokes. That's what all the trolls say.

JAMIE: Well, I'm not a troll. I was just trying to be funny.

SOPHIE: There's nothing funny about this, when you've experienced life like I have.

JAMIE:	I was different person back then. And even then they weren't sincere beliefs, I was just being…ironic.
SOPHIE:	Ironic?
JAMIE:	Yeah. When did everyone become so over sensitive?
SOPHIE:	You think I'm being oversensitive?
JAMIE:	Yeah, actually I do.
SOPHIE:	You've seen the abuse I get.
JAMIE:	I obviously meant being oversensitive about my tweets. But actually yeah you are being oversensitive.
SOPHIE:	Unbelievable.
JAMIE:	If someone is mean to you on the internet block them.
SOPHIE:	I get hundreds of messages.
JAMIE:	Then delete the fucking app.
SOPHIE:	You need to delete those tweets.
JAMIE:	I don't need to do anything.
SOPHIE:	This affects both of us.
JAMIE:	There's no point in deleting them.
SOPHIE:	Deleting them shows people you're sorry.

JAMIE:	But I'm not sorry. Deleting them makes it seem like I have something to hide. Everyone says stupid things when they're teenagers, put some perspective on this.
SOPHIE:	I am doing. That's why I'm leaving. Maybe you should visit your parents? They must be worried about you.
JAMIE:	What's to worry about?
SOPHIE:	Jamie, we were all over the news. You have spoken to your parents?
JAMIE:	Yeah.
SOPHIE:	What did your Dad say?
JAMIE:	His mate isn't able to offer me that internship anymore.
SOPHIE:	About the selfie?
JAMIE:	Nothing, because there's nothing to talk about. It's not a big deal.
SOPHIE:	Yeah well, I got fired, so it's kind of a big deal to me.
JAMIE:	You should sue.
SOPHIE:	We don't all have barristers for parents. Do the right thing and say sorry.
JAMIE:	This isn't about doing the right thing. It's about looking like you're doing the right thing. That's what it's all about, flog you in

the street. Tar and feather you. It makes them feel like they're doing something meaningful. All they care about is making themselves feel good.

SOPHIE: So, you're just going to do nothing?

JAMIE: Why not? It's not like your idea is working out any better for you.

SOPHIE: You don't get it do you?

JAMIE: You keep acting like we're guilty. And we're not, that's why I won't delete the tweets, that's why I won't say sorry. It's the principle of the situation.

SOPHIE: This isn't a debate; this is my life.

JAMIE: It's just strangers on the internet, people you'll never meet. If anything happened in the real world/ we would.

SOPHIE: This is the real world. People say they're going to attack me and all you can say is ignore it.

JAMIE: I'm just trying to stay optimistic.

SOPHIE: Look Jamie, I've had way more abuse than you, but when these tweets go viral, you're going to go through so much shit. Not just you and me, your whole family. You need to forget your ego and delete them and show some remorse.

JAMIE:	If I do that, the trolls win. If you go to your Mum's the trolls win. We need to stay and fight, together.
SOPHIE:	I don't want to fight; I want to be somewhere I can feel safe.
JAMIE:	I can keep you safe.
SOPHIE:	No, you can't.
JAMIE:	Don't give into the mob.
SOPHIE:	Get out of my way.
JAMIE:	Look sleep on it. If you still feel like you want to go in / the morning.
SOPHIE:	Jamie, get out of my way.
JAMIE:	Running away won't make this any better.
SOPHIE:	I can't stay here, not if you're not going to delete those tweets.
JAMIE:	It was your idea to take that selfie.
SOPHIE:	I'll finish packing in my room.

Sophie zips up the suitcase and exits.

Jamie pulls out his phone. Holds it up like he is taking a selfie. The following is addressed to the phone.

JAMIE:	Hello, my name is Jamie Gilmore. You might not know who I am but I'm pretty certain you've seen my face. Zombiegate. You've all seen it. All quietly judged me and

my best friend. Well now it's my turn to judge you. You bunch of whining, hypocritical, knee jerk, reactionary, self-proclaimed guardians of moral standards. Anyone with half a brain cell can see. Anyone who bothered to stop and think before smashing their fat fingers across a keyboard can see that the photo is clearly not meant to insult. We were on our way to a fancy-dress party. On Halloween. We'd taken the time to dress up, did you really think we spent all that time and money, so we could go and mock the death of a child we'd never even met? No that would be insane. We didn't see the flowers. Not because as some of you have suggested because we were too busy looking at our own reflection. Because it was dark. Our minds were on other things. This whole thing has been blown out of proportion by snowflakes looking to be offended.

My friend was fired. She loved that job. Every single person who signed that petition, shared that photo, or used that hashtag is responsible for what happened to her. You all shamed her. Well shame on you. You were all so quick to judge and jump to conclusions when we did something you saw to be wrong. But where was the moral outrage when people sent her death threats, why was no one offended by people threating to rape her? Where were the petitions for those people to be fired? Nowhere, because you don't care about doing the right thing, you just want to look like you're doing the right thing. I know, there are people who are planning to attack me. Claiming I sent some "racists" tweets. Think you've got some dirt on me? I don't care. Bring it. Because you're just bullies hiding behind your laptops. I won't be afraid of you. Shame me all you want. I'll fight back. As for the rest of you. If you're not part of the solution, you're part of the problem. If you agree with me, use the hashtag Jamie is Right. Ciao Amigos.

Jamie holds his phone for a moment clicks send.

The sound of notifications fills the space.

Lights on the Punch & Judy Booth, The Devil appears.

DEVIL: Hey man, really love your video.

JAMIE: Oh thanks.

DEVIL: Yeah, really like how you stick to the Woke Stassi. People are too easily offended these days.

JAMIE: Exactly.

DEVIL: All those liberal elites saying, "You can't listen to that song because it's problematic." "You can't read that book because it's racist." "You can't watch that film because it was directed by a sexual predator." Where is it all going to end?

JAMIE: Well, I'm not sure that's the same as what happened to us.

DEVIL: It is. It all comes back to same thing, suppress freedom of thought, freedom of expression. Make sure everybody thinks the same way.

JAMIE: Sorry, who are you?

DEVIL: I'm your data profiler, I look at everything you do online and then find products, websites, and other content that we think will be of interest to you.

JAMIE: You track everything I do online?

DEVIL: Yeah.

JAMIE: Bit creepy.

DEVIL: It's all in the terms and conditions. Besides it's perfectly harmless, you see adverts all the time. Isn't it better that they are adverts tailor made for you?

JAMIE: I guess, so what do you think I'll like?

DEVIL: Things like "Woke students want to rewrite history" "Me Too might have good intentions but they'll destroy capitalism" and "the truth about the Holocaust."

JAMIE: Wait, what was that last one?

DEVIL: Why don't you have a look and see for yourself? It's a free country, for now.

Jamie looks at his phone, lights fade.

EIGHT

Lights up on Booth Punch and Clown enter

PUNCH: Look boyz and girlz it's Joey the clown.

CLOWN: Actually, I've rebranded I'm now Clownface85.

PUNCH: Oh hello, Clownface85

CLOWN: Have you seen Jamie is right?

PUNCH: What's that?

CLOWN: The guy from the Zombiegate selfie, he's made a video refusing to say sorry.

PUNCH: Those guys are the worst.

CLOWN: He's made a video calling the haters out and saying people overacted.

PUNCH: Overacted? Overacted? Overeacted?

Punch gets his slapstick and hits Clown.

Is that an overaction?

CLOWN: It is a little bit. This Jamie is Right is actually really funny.

PUNCH: What's funny about mocking dead children?

CLOWN: It's quite clear they weren't doing that.

PUNCH: What about his racist tweets?

CLOWN:	He was a teenager; we all make mistakes. Hashtag Jamie is Right.

Social media notification

JAMIE:	Jamie Gilmore just posted a new video. 'Do we really need so many disabled parking spaces?'
CLOWN:	Lol this guy is amazing hashtag Jamie is Right.
PUNCH:	First dead kids now the disabled, where does this guy get off?
CLOWN:	Hang on your Mr Punch, you love having fun at other people's expense.
PUNCH:	This is different!
CLOWN:	How?
PUNCH:	Because he's not funny and I am.
JAMIE:	Jamie Gilmore just posted a new video. 'No, me saying ciao amigos isn't cultural appropriation.'

Punch begins to hit Clown, Clown fights back.

JAMIE:	Jamie Gilmore just posted a new video. 'I know how to solve the Insulate Britain protest, run them over!"
CLOWN:	Lolz. 20,000 views. This guy is the best. So funny and so true. Really glad he's sticking it to all the haters.

PUNCH: Sod this.

Punch exits

JAMIE: Jamie Gilmore just posted a new video. 'Who are the real fascists? People making Nazis jokes, or the people telling you what you can and can't say?'

CLOWN: 1 million views. Absolute legend. Jamie is right, Jamie is right.

Clown exits

Policeman and Judy enter

JUDY: Officer, officer. I'd like to report a crime.

POLICEMAN: Ello, ello, ello, what's going on here?

JUDY: My husband, violently attacked me and my baby.

POLICEMAN: Leave this to me.

Policeman exits. Devil enters.

DEVIL: Hello, we noticed you were talking about babies, here are some baby products you might be interested in. Would you like to buy a baby chair, baby food, baby bid?

JUDY: No.

DEVIL: Baby bib with a picture of Nicholas Cage on it.

JUDY: No, my baby is dead.

DEVIL: Would you like a baby zombie fancy dress costume.

JUDY: Go away!

Devil exits. Policeman re-enters.

POLICEMAN: Thank you for registering these events with us, we have carefully reviewed all the evidence and have come to the conclusion that none of our terms of use have been breached.

JUDY: But he killed my baby!

POLICEMAN: Would you like to read our guide on how to avoid your baby being killed in the future?

JUDY: I'm the victim of a crime what are you going to do about it?

POLICEMAN: Your safety remains our utmost priority. Was this answer useful?

JUDY: No.

POLICEMAN: How would you rate your experience with us today?

Judy exits, Policeman follows.

Town Crier enters new app notification

TOWN C: Breaking News! Breaking News! Jamie Gilmore to begin speaking tour at colleges across the USA.

CLOWN: Jamie is right, Jamie is right, Jamie is right!

TOWN C: Calls for Jamie Gilmore's speaking tour at College campus to be cancelled, after his racist and ablest remarks.

CLOWN: Snowflakes trying to silence his free speech.

TOWN C: Jamie Gilmore to launch podcast! If you ask me taking that selfie was the best thing he ever did.

BOTH: Jamie is right! Jamie is right! Jamie is right! Jamie is right! Jamie is right! Jamie is right!

Blackout

NINE

A coffee shop Marcia and Jamie are sat at a table.

MARICA: The show is a hit.

JAMIE: That's great.

MARICA: There's a heat on you at the moment, a real momentum and we've got to strike whilst the iron is hot, run the whole nine yards, y'know the drill.

JAMIE: Mixing your metaphors.

MARICA: That's why you're the wordsmith. Pitch me the next episode.

JAMIE: Well, I have a few ideas, there's this spoken word artist I know, his first pamphlet is being released / and I think my listeners.

MARICA: Spoken word artists aren't big and impactful!

JAMIE: I know it doesn't sound exciting, but I really / like it and I think.

MARICA: Jamie is right isn't about you though. It's about your audience, what do they care about?

JAMIE: They're thoughtful intelligent people.

MARICA: They hate cancel culture; they hate woke snowflakes.

JAMIE: They're interested in ideas.

MARICA: Ideas, that are shocking and taboo.

JAMIE: Not always.

MARICA: What do you know about David L Fleming?

JAMIE: The Neo-Nazi?

MARICA: He prefers the term paleoconservative.

JAMIE: Yeah, but everyone else calls him a Nazi.

MARICA: He's a fan of your show.

JAMIE: What? Why?

MARICA: You're a free speech champion, a free thinker. He's seen your stuff and he wants to reach out. You're very popular with the Alt-Right.

JAMIE: I know but I've always seen myself as a more of liberal. I hate that so many people today get overly offended by things that don't matter. But Fleming, he's a proper racist.

MARICA: I thought you were against childish name calling.

JAMIE: Didn't he call for a Muslim ban in Europe?

MARICA: I'm not saying you have to agree with him on everything. But you do believe he has a right to voice his opinions?

JAMIE: Yeah, I guess.

MARICA: So, why not on your show?

JAMIE: Because it will look like, I'm endorsing those views.

MARICA: No, it will look like you're not afraid to challenge him. If he doesn't go on your show, he'll just do his own, where he gets to say what he wants completely unchallenged. If he's a guest, you can put the counter argument to him. Isn't that what you believe? All views should be debated in the marketplace of ideas.

JAMIE: I don't know, I'm not some shock jock. I want to do real journalism.

MARICA: Exactly, that's what this is. Your chance to scrutinise him, speak truth to power.

JAMIE: Won't the sponsors freak out?

MARICA: There are other ways to finance the podcast.

JAMIE: Like what?

MARICA: I've been approached by a group called the Oswald Institute, they're very interested in you and are keen for you to meet David. They think you would get along.

JAMIE: The Oswald Institute?

MARICA: It's a Think Tank, with very deep pockets.

JAMIE:	Yeah, I'm not sure that this is the right road for me. I think they and Fleming have a right to a platform, but I'm not sure that's the direction I want my podcast to go in. I'm going to the States in a few weeks maybe that will give the show a boost.
MARICA:	Well, you did manage to get yourself no platformed from most US Colleges, which to be fair is great P.R. Oh also The Telegraph are running a segment for Father's Day, getting notable people to interview their fathers about the big issues, they want to know if you'd be interested.
JAMIE:	No.
MARICA:	Well, check with your Dad, see what he says.
JAMIE:	He won't want to do it.
MARICA:	It's going to be for the Saturday magazine it will be a really nice piece.
JAMIE:	No!

Jamie's raised voice has shocked Marcia.

	My parents are very private people, he won't want to do it. Trust me.
MARICA:	Fine, let's talk when you get back from the States, see how you feel about everything then. I'm just trying to do what best for you. I really think you'd benefit from having David on your show, but if you don't want

him, you'll have to come with something
more impressive than a spoken word artist.

JAMIE: Something like my first video responding to
Zombiegate?

MARICA: I mean that would be incredible.

JAMIE: Ok, I might have an idea.

Blackout

TEN

In the Punch and Judy booth Crocodile is listening to a podcast.
Punch enters with some sausages.

PUNCH:	Oi! Crocodile! Crocodile! CROCODILE!
CROC:	What?
PUNCH:	I've got some sausages. Want to fight over them?
CROC:	No. I'm busy, listening to the new Jamie is Right podcast.
PUNCH:	Why would you want to listen to that shit? Guy's an arsehole.
CROC:	He's actually got some really interesting views. And he's actually funny unlike some people we know.
PUNCH:	What's that supposed to mean?
CROC:	Maybe, I'm bored of being taunted with sausages to then get beaten up by you.
PUNCH:	Typical little cry baby millennial.
CROC:	This guy is actually really smart; I figure you'd like him if you gave him a chance.
PUNCH:	He's an arsehole and so is she.
CROC:	Who?
PUNCH:	Sophie Cooper, she's a horrible little bitch.

CROC: Oh, does she also have a podcast?

PUNCH: Not yet, but I bet she will at some point.

CROC: Well, I doubt it will be as funny as this.

PUNCH: I'll show you funny.

Punch attacks Crocodile until the Crocodile is dead.

> Get up. I said get up I didn't hit you that hard. Crocodile? Come on this is what we do. We fight over sausages, it's just a joke. A joke we do.

He realises he's killed Crocodile.

> Look what they made me do. Bloody Zombiegate, they put me under so much stress. They keep pushing me and pushing me first Judy leaves me and now look what's happened. It's taken over everything. I'll make them pay for this.

Blackout

ELEVEN

A conservatory Jennifer sits at a table on laptop a printer by her feet.

JEN: Cannot connect to printer. It's over there. Maybe I need a wire? Sophie? Sophie? Printer is on the blink again!

Sophie enters still wearing her pyjamas and dressing gown.

SOPHIE: What?

JEN: It's the printer love, it says it cannot connect. Do you think it needs a wire? It didn't come with a wire/ should it have one?

SOPHIE: Its wireless.

JEN: Well, it won't connect.

SOPHIE: Honestly, it's not complicated.

Sophie leans over Jennifer and sends something to print. Nothing happens.

Well, it should be printing. Have you installed the software?

JEN: The printer has got ink, I put a new cartridge in.

SOPHIE: No, that's not the problem. Right move.

JEN: Don't be like/ that.

SOPHIE: I'll do it. You need to install new software.

JEN: Well the man in the shop didn't say/
anything.

SOPHIE: Move.

JEN: Are you sure it doesn't need a wire?

Sophie forces Jennifer out of the seat and begins to type away on her laptop.

Mr Punch enters the booth with a phone, he dials

JEN: Do you want a brew?

SOPHIE: I'm fine.

The phone rings Jennifer answers.

JEN: Hello?

PUNCH: Hollo? Hollo?

JEN: Who is this?

PUNCH: *(singing)* Ugly witch,

Gave birth to Zombiegate bitch,

Should have had an abortion.

JEN: Who is this?

PUNCH: That's the way to do it!

JEN: I've told you before stop calling us. I'm
reporting you to the police.

Jennifer hangs up the phone, Mr Punch laughs and disappears.

JEN:	I'm calling 1471.
SOPHIE:	There's no point.
JEN:	Withheld number bastard!
SOPHIE:	What did he say?
JEN:	One day he's going to screw up and then we'll catch him.
SOPHIE:	What did he say?
JEN:	It was vulgar, I'm not repeating it.
SOPHIE:	He's probably sent me worse.
JEN:	Well, I'm reporting it.
SOPHIE:	What's the point the police never do anything?
JEN:	I was thinking of going for a walk later, do you want to come?
SOPHIE:	I don't think that's a good idea.
JEN:	Why's that?
SOPHIE:	I'm not exactly very popular at the moment am I?
JEN:	I just meant around the village. I doubt anyone around here has even heard of it.
SOPHIE:	Mum, it was in the local paper.
JEN:	Well, it wasn't really about you was it. It was about Jamie's podcast.

SOPHIE: It's got our names in the article.

JEN: I'm sure nobody noticed that, it was mainly about him interviewing that local footballer who punched that photographer. He's looking very trim in the photo.

SOPHIE: Mum!

JEN: What? He did seem very angry. Was he always like that?

SOPHIE: Yes, no. Sometimes.

JEN: Apparently his tour in the US is getting protested.

SOPHIE: Can't say I'm surprised after the things he's said.

JEN: Well, obviously I don't agree with a lot of the things he says. But then we do have freedom of speech. If you don't like what someone's say you should challenge them not silence them.

SOPHIE: Silence him? You can't shut him up, he's everywhere! Podcast, YouTube, even in the bloody Cheshire Gazette. Meanwhile I'm sat here unemployed.

JEN: Well, I doubt any of this stuff matters in the long run. Tomorrow's chip paper that's what we use to call the newspaper.

SOPHIE: Accept it's not now is it? It's kept on a
                database somewhere, kept forever.

JEN: Yes, but there's so much of it these days,
                people will forget.

SOPHIE: Punch doesn't.

Beat

                Well, it looks like your printer will be up and
                running in…

Sophie clicks a few buttons. Nothing happens.

                Cannot connect to printer. What do you
                mean? You're fucking connected. I just
                fucking…

JEN: Does it need a wire?

SOPHIE: It's wireless.

JEN: So, about this walk.

SOPHIE: You should get blinds in here.

JEN: Why would I want to get blinds in here?

SOPHIE: To help keep out the light.

JEN: The whole reason I had the conservatory
                built was so I could get more light.

SOPHIE: I hate conservatories.

JEN: You've never complained about it before.

SOPHIE: I've never really thought about it.

JEN:	Well, it's built now. If you had a complaint, you should have written to the council, when I applied for planning permission.
SOPHIE:	I mean doesn't it bother you? You're sat surrounded by glass. What if it was to smash?
JEN:	It's double glazing. It's not going to smash.
SOPHIE:	Earthquakes.
JEN:	What?
SOPHIE:	If there was an Earthquake. You'd be cut to pieces.
JEN:	I'm more concerned about birds crapping on the roof.
SOPHIE:	You're completely on show here. Anyone could see you.
JEN:	It's the back garden.
SOPHIE:	Anyone could be watching.
JEN:	What's brought this on?
SOPHIE:	I just think you need to be safer.
JEN:	You're being paranoid.
SOPHIE:	Am I? People have drones now.
JEN:	Drones?

SOPHIE:	Yeah. Drones. Robot planes with cameras on. They could fly over and film you sat in here. There could be a drone up there. Right now. Watching us. And we wouldn't even see it.
JEN:	Well now you're being ridiculous.
SOPHIE:	What did he say?
JEN:	Who?
SOPHIE:	Punch.
JEN:	I'm not repeating it. It's disgusting.
SOPHIE:	Well yeah. He's a troll. That's what he does.
JEN:	No this is beyond trolling now. It's been months and he's still calling. Doesn't matter what you do he's still able to find you. I mean how did he get our landline?
SOPHIE:	Was probably able to work it out after he saw the story in the gazette.
JEN:	He's read the gazette; you think he's local?
SOPHIE:	No Mum, it's on the gazette website, anyone in the world could see that article if they wanted to.
JEN:	Madness. How about this walk?
SOPHIE:	Sure, let me just finish connecting the printer.

JEN:	I can do that later.
SOPHIE:	No, you can't.
JEN:	I managed to install Zoom all by myself.
SOPHIE:	Yeah, and the way you go on about anyone would think you hacked into the Pentagon. OK, let's try again.

Sophie sends something to print. Nothing happens.

Fucking useless piece of shit.

Sophie kicks the printer.

JEN:	Sophie!
SOPHIE:	I've fucking done everything it wants me to do. I've done, I've done, I've done it – but still nothing works. I'm still trapped.
JEN:	It's only the printer love.
SOPHIE:	No, it's everything I do. Can't get a job, can't have any friends, can't even get the printer to work. That's all I'm going to be that girl who took that selfie, that stupid zombiegate bitch.
JEN:	It's going to be OK.
SOPHIE:	Do you remember when we were poor?
JEN:	Is that the problem you need money?
SOPHIE:	No, no it's not that. Just I miss us being poor.

JEN: Well, that's because you can't remember it as well as I do.

SOPHIE: I remember when you'd come in after college. You'd be out the door within 45 minutes.

JEN: Look perhaps it's for the best, you've no longer got that job. There's more to life than work. When you first started working there you told me it was going to be a temporary thing. You were going to go travelling.

SOPHIE: Yeah, but then I found something I was really good at.

JEN: You're good at lots of things.

Beat

I'm sorry I wasn't around more when you were growing up. You understand why? I was trying to make things better, make life better for us.

SOPHIE: Yeah. I understand. I loved those forty odd minutes though. When it was just the two of us, no Grandma, or babysitters, just us two. School, work, none of that mattered we just spent time together. I always thought if I worked hard, if I applied myself, got a good job. I'd be alright.

JEN: And you will be. We all hit bumps along the way. God knows I did.

SOPHIE:	Were you ever fired?
JEN:	No, thankfully.
SOPHIE:	What would you have done? If what happened to me had happened to you?
JEN:	I don't know. I guess I would have gone back and lived with Grandma and Grandad.
SOPHIE:	They would have hated that.
JEN:	They would have helped me. Because that's what parents do.
SOPHIE:	I guess it's something they didn't have to worry about. You never fucked up.
JEN:	Yes, I did. Everybody does.
SOPHIE:	Everyone doesn't end up with a petition to get them fired.
JEN:	You were unlucky. But you've got brains. I know it doesn't feel like it now. But you'll get back on your feet. You're a survivor. You get it from me. Jamie's been able to get back on his feet, I'm sure you will to.
SOPHIE:	Wait.

Sophie searches something on the internet.

> That's it. Jamie, that's why we keep being trolled. The phone calls, the abuse it always spikes whenever he's trending. Podcasts, video, pieces in the Gazette. Yeah of course

82

he posted a new video last night. Look there
he is in the comments.

JEN: I thought you said you deleted all your social
media accounts?

SOPHIE: I have this is just an anonymous account to
keep an eye on things.

JEN: I'm not sure that's a good idea.

SOPHIE: I know what I'm doing.

JEN: Let's do something else away from the
computer. Let's go out this evening take our
mind of things. We could go for a meal or the
cinema?

SOPHIE: Don't you have one of your committee
meetings?

JEN: No, not tonight.

SOPHIE: It's the first Wednesday of the month, you
always have a/ meeting on.

JEN: I've decided to take a little break from the
committee.

SOPHIE: You're quitting, why?

JEN: I'm not quitting. I made that clear. I said
"I'm not quitting". But I've decided to take
a back seat.

SOPHIE: Why?

JEN: Well, I've got a lot on my plate. I'm very busy.

SOPHIE: You like being busy?

JEN: And to spend more time with you.

SOPHIE: Have they forced you?

JEN: No. Don't be daft. I'm just taking a break. Until you get back on your feet.

SOPHIE: Have they forced you out because of the selfie.

JEN: No, no. But Claire is right. You're home. You need me more than the committee does. I haven't resigned. Not formally.

SOPHIE: Because of what was in the paper?

JEN: It really isn't a big deal. But I'm free tonight, if you want to go out?

SOPHIE: I think I'd rather stay in.

JEN: Sure I can't twist your arm?

SOPHIE: Maybe. No, look let me fix the printer and then see how I am?

JEN: Great.

SOPHIE: I've got stuff to do Mum.

JEN: Forget about the printer.

SOPHIE: Not just that, I've got job applications to do.
You go for your walk, I don't mind.

JEN: Well, you really should leave the house, not
natural to spend all day indoors.

SOPHIE: Alright, alright.

JEN: Love you.

SOPHIE: Love you too.

*Jennifer exits. Sophie begins to furiously type away on the laptop,
she's on to something.*

Blackout

TWELVE

Jamie and Chuck in a recording studio, Punch in booth is listening in.

CHUCK: Welcome back to Truth Bomb, with me your host, Chuck Dune, today I'm so stoked for our guest. This guy is incredible, I love him, I think you guys are going to love him. Please welcome to the show internet personality, rabble rouser and close personal friend of mine, Jamie Gilmore, welcome.

JAMIE: Thanks for having me on the show.

CHUCK: Now depending on who you speak to, Jamie Gilmore is either the Messiah or a very a naughty boy. Which is it Jamie?

JAMIE: Well, your listeners will have to think for themselves, won't they?

CHUCK: Good point. So, your rise to fame really has been incredible. 6 months ago, Jamie is Right, didn't even exist. And now you're one of the most talked about influencers.

JAMIE: I mean, I wouldn't call myself an influencer. I'm more of journalist.

CHUCK: Sure, sure. There's so much I want to talk to you about, but I guess we need to start at the beginning with that zombie selfie. I know you're probably sick to death of talking about it.

JAMIE: No, I love talking about it.

CHUCK: I mean I've read a lot of interviews with you, don't worry I do my research. But something I've been thinking about is, do you regret it?

JAMIE: That's a good question... No, I don't regret it. I think what that selfie did was it showed everyone what this outrage mill is all about. People like to be offended. They want to be outraged; they get a kick out of it. It's a tribal thing you know, us vs them. And look before that selfie, I was probably guilty of it myself. When you're on social media and you join in you get the likes, you get a shit tone of endorphins, it feels good. You feel powerful and I think the anger about that selfie was so over the top, I think we exposed the stupidity of being offended. So I'm glad we took the selfie, I'm glad you were offended, now grow up. That's why we did it.

CHUCK: Wow hold up, did you just say "why we did it"? Are you saying you took the selfie on purpose?

JAMIE: Err, look it doesn't matter why we did it.

CHUCK: Was it on purpose?

JAMIE: Yeah, so what if it was on purpose? It was our Instagram feed we can post what we want.

CHUCK: Wow. That is quite the scoop for Truth Bomb, we'll be discussing this bombshell after these words from our sponsors.

Lights fade on Chuck and Jamie.

PUNCH: I knew it! They did it on purpose!

Lights fade on booth.

THIRTEEN

Jamie's flat.

SOPHIE:	What the fuck is wrong with you?
JAMIE:	You're making it sound worse than it is.
SOPHIE:	We did it on purpose?
JAMIE:	I didn't say that, well I did, but you have to put these things in a context.
SOPHIE:	Context?
JAMIE:	Yeah, have you listened to the podcast?
SOPHIE:	No, I haven't listened to your fucking podcast.
JAMIE:	Well, that's one of the points I was trying to make, you can't just cherry pick.
SOPHIE:	Don't talk to me like that?
JAMIE:	Like what?
SOPHIE:	Like I'm one of your stupid fans.
JAMIE:	They're not stupid.
SOPHIE:	Every single time that selfie gets mentioned I get fresh load of abuse.
JAMIE:	I know, it's exactly the same for me.
SOPHIE:	No, it's not. For you it's publicity.

Beat

JAMIE:	I wasn't aware you were still getting abuse.
SOPHIE:	We can't all be internet celebrities.
JAMIE:	I'm more of a journalist than a celebrity.
SOPHIE:	Well, I'm just Sophie Cooper and I want to be able to live my life without me and Mum getting abuse every time you start trending.
JAMIE:	You're Mum is getting abuse?
SOPHIE:	That Punch troll, got hold of her phone number.
JAMIE:	Ah well speaking of that guy.
SOPHIE:	I was on my way here when I got a phone call from a journalist asking me if it's true we planned the selfie.
JAMIE:	What did you say?
SOPHIE:	I just hung up.
JAMIE:	That's probably for the best. Do you want to get something to eat? I'm doing a special birthday livestream for my subscribers at nine.
SOPHIE:	Oh my god. Your birthday, I completely forgot.
JAMIE:	I thought that's why you were coming round?
SOPHIE:	No.

Beat

JAMIE: It's good to see you again.

SOPHIE: Same.

JAMIE: Hey, do you want to be in the livestream?

SOPHIE: No, thanks. I can't stay late. I've got to get the train back to Mum's.

JAMIE: Are you sure, you can crash on the sofa?

SOPHIE: No, I've got a job interview in the morning.

JAMIE: Cool, doing PR again?

SOPHIE: No, for a temp agency.

JAMIE: It's a shame my fans would have loved to meet you.

SOPHIE: Not really my scene.

JAMIE: What makes you say that?

SOPHIE: Politics for start.

JAMIE: Hey, my fans are free thinkers you'll find that there's quite a lot of diversity of opinion.

SOPHIE: I thought diversity was a dirty word in the Alt Right.

JAMIE: Don't say that.

SOPHIE: What I thought that was what you call yourself now.

JAMIE:	I don't use labels. Labels divide people. I'm just asking questions, pointing out absurdities, I'm a journalist.
SOPHIE:	A journalist who got themselves no platformed from / colleges across.
JAMIE:	Don't you start as well. I've already had an ear full from Mum.
SOPHIE:	How are things with your parents?
JAMIE:	Bad. Dad cut me off. He says what I'm doing is vulgar. Which is bullshit because I know he agrees with me on half the stuff I say, just thinks its uncouth to broadcast it. You know what he said when I told him how many podcast listeners I had? "Better to remain silent and be thought a fool than to speak and to remove all doubt."
SOPHIE:	I'm sorry Jamie.
JAMIE:	It's fine, he never understood me, not really. Not like you do.
SOPHIE:	Yeah, we we're friends.
JAMIE:	Best friends.
SOPHIE:	Sure. But now you have thousands of friends who hang on your every word.
JAMIE:	Yeah, but none of them actually want to spend time with me. Not the real me. They want this character I've created. Someone

who is always outrageous, always witty, always saying the unsayable. Y'know the morning after the photo/ I was going tell you something.

SOPHIE: Sorry, I need to say something. I think the reason I'm still getting trolled, is because of you.

JAMIE: What?

SOPHIE: Every time, you say something outrageous or controversial, the abuse starts again.

JAMIE: You're really pissed about that podcast?

SOPHIE: Yeah, I am. It was a lie, a dangerous lie which puts me and my Mum in danger.

JAMIE: Danger? I think you / might be.

SOPHIE: Let me finish. We are both in that photo what you say about it, what you do, affects both of us and only one of us benefits from it.

JAMIE: Do you think maybe the people sending you the abuse are the ones in the wrong?

SOPHIE: Of course, but if you weren't doing what you were doing.

JAMIE: For once in my life, I'm actually successful.

SOPHIE: I just wish you would think of me for a change.

JAMIE:	Think of you? I'm always thinking of you. You're the one who ran away.
SOPHIE:	I was getting death threats.
JAMIE:	We both were, we could have handled it together.
SOPHIE:	It wasn't the same for you. We were treated differently.
JAMIE:	Yeah, because you said sorry.
SOPHIE:	That is not the reason.
JAMIE:	That's the thing that separates us.
SOPHIE:	You're a straight white man, that's the difference.
JAMIE:	Oh, don't start with all that identity politics bullshit.
SOPHIE:	You've lived your whole life in a privileged bubble.
JAMIE:	That's not fair, you know I struggled for years to get a break. Whilst everyone else I knew kept rising and rising.
SOPHIE:	Because we were actually doing the work. You struggled because you were waiting for something to be handed over to you. I worked so hard to get that job and then it was snatched away from me.
JAMIE:	You lost your job, so I should lose mine?

SOPHIE:	No, but I lose my job, you get a podcast, you don't honestly think we were treated the same?
JAMIE:	You weren't treated differently because of who you are.
SOPHIE:	Then what was it about?
JAMIE:	It's about how you deal with the internet. You gave in too soon. If you'd held in longer.
SOPHIE:	Hold in? For how long? Till they broke into my house and raped me?
JAMIE:	They wouldn't. That was just an idle threat.
SOPHIE:	How do you know that?
JAMIE:	Did anyone ever break into our flat?
SOPHIE:	Oh, fuck this.

Sophie goes to leave.

JAMIE:	I do think about you. Every day. In fact, my next video is all about you.
SOPHIE:	I don't want to be in one of your crappy videos.
JAMIE:	I found Mr Punch.
SOPHIE:	What?
JAMIE:	The troll, Mr Punch I found out who he really is.

SOPHIE:	How?
JAMIE:	I got talking to these troll hunter guys, they worked out who he is.
SOPHIE:	You're serious.
JAMIE:	Have a look for yourself.

He hands her a tablet.

	Facebook profile, LinkedIn, even found out what school his sister teaches at. Mental what you can find out online.
SOPHIE:	This can't be him.
JAMIE:	No, it is, he's very clever masking his IP address VPNs all of that type of thing, but they found an old tweet from 2013 complaining about the bins to the local council, complete with a photo, house number written on the bin, a quick google earth search and bingo, the rest just fell into place.
SOPHIE:	His profile picture though?
JAMIE:	Oh, apparently that's his thing marathon running, he's a big marathon runner.
SOPHIE:	He's wearing a Wishing Well T-Shirt.
JAMIE:	Oh shit, so he is.

SOPHIE:	We only give those to people who do fundraising for us. He ran the marathon for Wishing Well.
JAMIE:	Shit.
SOPHIE:	Do you think that's why he?
JAMIE:	Doesn't matter how many fun runs he's done Soph, doesn't excuse what he's done.
SOPHIE:	Yeah, you're right. So, have you taken this to the police?
JAMIE:	No, what are they going to do?
SOPHIE:	Trolling is a crime.
JAMIE:	What's the point? He'll get a suspended sentence and be back online within the year, doing this to someone else.
SOPHIE:	What did you mean about a video?
JAMIE:	What I said, a video exposing him.
SOPHIE:	You're going to shame him?
JAMIE:	Expose him.
SOPHIE:	How can you do that to someone after what we've been through? It's ruined our lives.
JAMIE:	He needs to be punished; he can't just be allowed to keep behaving like this.
SOPHIE:	Yeah, through the legal system.

JAMIE:	The legal system is run by people like my Dad.
SOPHIE:	I've got no problem with your little grift, if provoking people online is earning you a living good for you. But this, this is a real person's life it matters.
JAMIE:	It all matters, it's not a grift. Jamie is Right is about expressing myself.
SOPHIE:	It's about creating excuses because you don't want to say sorry.
JAMIE:	It's more than that. There's a lot of pressure on me.
SOPHIE:	From who?
JAMIE:	My agency. They've invested a lot of money into me, they're worried they won't see a return unless I appeal to a certain audience.
SOPHIE:	Like who?
JAMIE:	They want me to have a Neo-Nazi on my show.
SOPHIE:	You said no right?
JAMIE:	That's why I've made the Punch video. They need me to do something big to drive in listeners. Zombiegate is what created Jamie is Right, Zombiegate is what can save it and keep it as a serious piece of journalism.
SOPHIE:	You think this is serious journalism?

JAMIE:	It's a step in the right direction.
SOPHIE:	This is a man's life we're talking about.
JAMIE:	Yeah, a man who hates you. A man who sends abuse to your Mum. You should be thanking me, not lecturing me.
SOPHIE:	If you post that video online, I am leaving.
JAMIE:	It's too late. The video went live an hour ago.
SOPHIE:	Take it down. Take it down now.

Neither off them move for a beat.

Sophie goes to leave

JAMIE:	Wait! The morning we discovered we'd gone viral; I was going to tell you something.
SOPHIE:	What?
JAMIE:	I was going to tell you that I liked you. I still like you. Do you feel the same?
SOPHIE:	I didn't like you Jamie, I loved you. But the Jamie I loved would do anything for his friends, now look at you trying to impress a bunch of strangers on the internet. For a long time, I thought you made the right decision, but seeing you now. You're so lonely.

Sophie exits.

FOURTEEN

Lights on Booth. Judy and Policeman enter.

JUDY: Mr Punch is out of control, surely there's something you can do.

POLICEMAN: I'm afraid my hands of tied.

JUDY: He beat up my baby, attacked me and he's killed the crocodile and yet he faces no consequences for his actions. He's just running around singing "enjoy yourself". How long until he attacks someone else?

POLICEMAN: Hold up what did you just say?

JUDY: He killed the crocodile.

POLICEMAN: No, that bit about singing?

JUDY: He's singing the song "enjoy yourself".

POLICEMAN: That's copyright infringement! We take intellectual property very seriously.

JUDY: Does that mean you'll do something?

POLICEMAN: No. We still don't know who he is.

Judy exits

Town Crier enters new app notification

TOWN C: Breaking news! Breaking news! Notorious internet troll Mr Punch has been unmasked by internet star, Jamie is right. Mr Punch real name Tony Ford, who works as an IT

100

Specialist. Sent thousands of messages to people, mainly women, often threatening violence.

POLICEMAN: Ello, ello, ello. This looks like a job for me. Ne naw, ne naw, ne naw, ne naw.

Policeman and Town Crier exit.

Punch enters

PUNCH: *(sings)* Enjoy yourself, it's later than you think. Enjoy yourself.

Policeman enters

POLICEMAN: Ello, ello, ello Mr Punch we've had a few complaints you'll have to come with me.

PUNCH: You'll never take me alive.

Punch hits Policeman it has no affect on Policeman.

POLICEMAN: Stop that.

PUNCH: Never.

Punch exits, followed by Policeman.

Clown enters

CLOWN: Move out the way Punch, there's a new lord of misrule and his name is Jamie Gilmore. Jamie is right, Jamie is right, Jamie is right!

POLICEMAN: Have any of you seen Mr Punch?

Mr Punch appears outside the booth laughing, he then disappears

Oi! How did he get there?

Policeman and Clown exit

Punch enters

PUNCH: Run, run as fast as you can, you can't catch me I'm the...

Policeman appears and hits him, Punch collapses.

POLICEMAN: Alright, sunny Jim you're fuckin' nicked! Your days of acting out violence for entertainment are over.

PUNCH: Nicked! What have I done wrong?

POLICEMAN: You trolled Sophie Cooper, beat up your wife and the baby, killed the crocodile and worst of all infringed-on copyright law. Do you have anything to say for yourself?

PUNCH: I never said I was perfect, sure I've made mistakes, who hasn't? I never meant to hurt anyone, I'm sorry if some people feel offended by my actions. I'm an old puppet when I was growing up things were different. These days if you say abusive things, beat up your loved ones, torture and kill animals suddenly you're the bad guy. You know what I find scary the idea that me someone who is as English as Fish & Chips, Afternoon Tea and statues of slave traders, is being cancelled, that's Orwellian. I thought we were living in 2022 not 1984. When did we all become so oversensitive? What about freedom of speech? And if they come for old red nose, who is going to be next?

Policeman drags off Punch screaming.

Judy enters

JUDY: And so, ends our tragical comedy or comical tragedy of Mr Punch. There's a moral lesson for you all to learn and that is...

Town Crier rushes on

TOWN C: The court case of Mr Punch has been abandoned, after a member of the jury was caught live tweeting the court case. Whilst Mr Ford's defence argue that this is cause for a miss trial, prosecutors argue that justice must be served.

Town Crier exits

JUDY: This is getting ridiculous.

Town Crier Enters

TOWN C: The notorious internet troll known as Mr Punch was today sentenced to 2 years in prison for sending malicious electronic messages. A notorious troll who came to public attention after the so called Zombiegate scandal. Mr Punch real name Tony Ford was described as obsessive in his pursuit of Miss Cooper. The internet personality Jamie Gilmore who exposed Mr

Ford across his social media platforms, tweeted that justice had been delivered. Sophie Cooper was not available for comment.

JUDY: After all these years are we finally free from the abuse of Mr Punch?

TOWN C: Could I play Devil's Avocado for a moment? I don't agree with what Punch said or did. But isn't hearing things we don't want to hear, the price we must pay to live in a free and tolerant society?

JUDY: But a tolerant society cannot tolerate intolerance, for fear that the tolerant members of that society will be destroyed.

TOWN C: Oh, fuck off!

Town Crier and Judy pick up sticks and begin to hit one another, the slapstick violence carries on as the lights slowly fade on the puppet booth.

FIFTEEN

A prison visitor area, Tony sits on one side of a table wearing a hi-vis tabard, Sophie sits on the other side.

SOPHIE: Thank you for agreeing to meet with me. I have a couple of questions I wanted to ask you about everything.

TONY: I said all I had to say at the trial.

SOPHIE: You declined to give evidence.

TONY: It's weird seeing you without the zombie make up. The image in my head is that you always have that on. Funny that.

SOPHIE: Why did you do it?

TONY: Do what?

SOPHIE: The trolling.

TONY: I thought you deserved it for making fun of that dead child.

SOPHIE: We didn't make...that was a misunderstanding.

TONY: I don't believe you.

SOPHIE: It wasn't just me you abused, there were others.

TONY: And they all deserved it.

SOPHIE: Making mistakes on social media platforms warrants rape and death threats.

TONY: I never threated anyone.

SOPHIE: You threatened me.

TONY: I made jokes. Jokes at your expense? Sure. Cruel jokes? Sometimes. Jokes that were offensive? Absolutely. But that's all they were jokes.

SOPHIE: Pretty sick sense of humour.

TONY: Guilty. Trolls are the court jesters of the internet, they prick pomposity, satires, hold the feet of the powerful to flames of truth.

SOPHIE: But I wasn't powerful, I was a woman who did one thing wrong and then I'm being trolled with abuse and death threats, I was scared for my life.

TONY: Trolling isn't all about abuse.

SOPHIE: Feels like it.

TONY: Do you know why it's called trolling? I bet you think it's because of trolls from fairy tales. Horrible monsters hiding in the shadows, don't feed the trolls. Am I right?

SOPHIE: I guess.

TONY: Common mistake. Trolling is actually a fishing term. It's laying bait. That's the art of trolling, laying something down and waiting to see who will bite, who will take offence, who will fall into the trap.

SOPHIE:	But why? Surely you have better things to do with your time.
TONY:	It's funny. Trolling is as old as the internet, back in the day when we still had dial up modems. I'd be on messageboards winding people up with Python jokes, sure it was childish but it was also really fun.
SOPHIE:	Big leap from Python to threating to rape people.
TONY:	Internets a big place these days, got to shout a lot louder to be heard.
SOPHIE:	Is that why you did so much charity work? You felt guilty about trolling?
TONY:	I don't feel guilty about trolling.
SOPHIE:	What do you think Ava would say if she could see her Dad now?
TONY:	No. No don't you fucking dare, talk to me.
SOPHIE:	It's kind of scary how much you can find out with just a couple of details. Like all I need is your name, her name and quick Google search will tell me she received a Wishing Well grant.
TONY:	You have no right to pry into my family life.
SOPHIE:	You had no right sending abuse to my Mum! That's why you do it, isn't it? You're so angry at the world because of what

happened to your daughter you like to lash out at strangers on the internet. Abusing people like me online makes you feel good about your own pathetic life.

TONY: Is that your pop psychology assessment of me? It's nothing that dramatic. The internet is a space for everyone. A place where you can say and do anything. We don't want to be bossed around by Big Government or Big Tech. If there's a problem we'll handle it ourselves. You were a problem, we dealt with you.

SOPHIE: But even after I was fired, deleted my accounts, you still came after me. Why?

TONY: He showed no remorse and kept being rewarded. It made no sense.

SOPHIE: That wasn't me. If you were angry at him why send me abuse?

TONY: There's just something about you in that photo. Something that drove me mad.

SOPHIE: Because I'm a woman.

TONY: I like to think I chose Mr Punch as my avatar because I love his spirit of anarchy. The Lord of Misrule, the ultimate symbol of chaos. I think that's what trolling should be about, chaos and anarchy. Also the other thing I like about Punch is, he gets away with it. Do you know how the story of

108

Punch and Judy ends? In a traditional Punch and Judy show, like a proper Victorian one, none of this PC crap they do for kids now. In a proper Punch and Judy show, Mr Punch wins. He's sentenced to be hung. But he tricks the hangman into hanging himself, he tricks everyone even the devil. I figured as long as I was Mr Punch, I'd always get away with it.

Looks at his surroundings

Think I've fucked up.

SOPHIE: I don't agree with what Jamie did to you. I think that was cruel, I'm sorry that happened to you.

TONY: Is this the part where I say sorry? Because I'm not. Dragging you down felt like dragging down every spoilt millennial, your generation is always complaining, the first in line to bitch and moan about your feelings. But none of you brats have suffered, not real suffering. Never had your hearts broken, never had your entire world come tumbling down. You complain about global warming and capitalism whilst you pose for selfies on beaches on all four corners of the globe. So that's why I did it I wanted you to suffer, I wanted you to feel pain. And you know what, it felt good.

SOPHIE: You're now in prison for your misogynistic abuse, was it worth it?

TONY: Misogynistic? Honestly, there are actual murders in here. Rapists, men who beat up their wives and gloat about it. I said some mean things on the internet. You need some perspective. Learn to separate what happens in this world and what happens online.

SOPHIE: You can't separate them though. Whether you like it or not they're linked. I suffered in one because of another.

TONY: You weren't the only one.

SOPHIE: You're right, we've all experienced the same thing.

TONY: Have we? Because when we're done here, you get to leave I don't. How much money do you think Jamie made from that video about me?

SOPHIE: He didn't do it for money.

TONY: How much?

SOPHIE: The way he did things was wrong.

TONY: Was it? He's not the one sat in here, is he? No, he knows exactly what he's doing. Jamie is right, that's the way to do it.

Lights fade

SIXTEEN

Jamie in his flat filming a video, Sophie is in her room packing and watching the video on her phone.

JAMIE: Hi amigos, Jamie here. Got some pretty exciting news, next week will be the 100th episode of the Jamie is Right podcast! Pretty exciting right? And to celebrate, we are going to be joined by a very special guest, the one and only David L Fleming. Not only do we have an incredible guest, but we're also going to be livestreaming it. Our first ever live podcast, it's happening next Wednesday 9pm GMT 5pm EST. Not only do we have an incredible guest and our first ever live show. This special celebration is in partnership with the Oswald Institute, an incredible organisation doing great work, tune in next week and I'll tell you all about them and all the really kickass stuff we've got planned for you guys.

I just want to take this opportunity to say thank you to you all. I have the best fans in the world, so many of you listen to the podcast every week, and that means so much to me. Y'know sometimes doing Jamie is Right feels more like a movement than a show, feels like we're building something special. Recently someone called me lonely. But I'm not am I? Because I've got all you guys, listening, watching, messaging me from all over the world. That's the great thing about social media it brings us all together, thousands of us connecting. Doesn't matter where I am, what I'm going through, who in my "real life" has let me down. I know that there are thousands of people who care about me, who support me, who believe in me, who are all just an app away.

Jennifer enters, Sophie pauses the video. Jamie pauses.

JEN: The taxi's here. Are you ready?

SOPHIE: Yes.

JEN: And you have everything you need?

SOPHIE: Yes.

JEN: Passport?

SOPHIE: Yes.

JEN: Tickets?

SOPHIE: Mum, I'm going to be fine.

JEN: I know. I'm so proud of you.

They hug.

The taxi beeps its horn.

Right, come on.

Jennifer exits. Sophie clicks play. Jamie continues.

JAMIE: This has been a really wild ride and nobody can ever know what the future holds, but I've got a feeling with fans like you the future is going to be pretty incredible. So, until next time Ciao Amigos!

Sophie places her phone in her pocket and exits.

Jamie sits alone.

He checks his phone for notifications – nothing.

Puts it down.

He checks again – nothing.

Puts it down.

He checks again – still nothing

Lights slowly fade.

THE END